Automotive Restorers Guide

For Cars & Motorcycles
Veteran, Vintage, Classic & Custom

1st Edition

SW Barratt

www.automotiverestorersguide.com

SB Helpful Media. ISBN 9781838132347

Disclaimer: This book is sold as information only. Whilst every effort has been made in writing this guide book the author and publishers are not responsible for any personal loss or liability caused by using information contained herein, or if a company listed should cease trading.

Affiliate Disclaimer: The author of this eBook may receive a commission for recommendations made to Heritage Insurance. For example, if the link is used and a purchase made then the author would receive a commission. The recommendation reflect the fact that the author has either used or researched the company to ensure that they provide an independent, approved value for money service to customers. The author would not promote the services otherwise, as this guide book is written to give genuine help and advice.

Index

Introduction

As many vintage, classic car and motorcycle enthusiasts often find is that searching for restoration services is nearly always a long tedious task trying to find a decent specialist service. You are often not sure about the reliability of the person or company you are dealing with.

The following guide aims to provide the reader with a list of some useful services, which over the years have provided a decent service at a fair price. An index to the guide is located on pages iii and iv.

Some of the services listed in the guide can also supply parts. This can be very useful when your main dealer or another supplier may say that they can no longer supply what you are looking for.

For example, your main dealer or supplier may say that the only way to get the piston rings is to purchase new pistons complete with the rings! T&L Engineering listed in the guide can often supply piston rings, valves, bearings, gaskets, etc.

The guide is listed in alphabetical order for easy reference. Some companies are listed more than once, but this is to make finding a service easier.

About the Author

SW Barratt

Steve Barratt with the classic 'Cosmic Wheels' 6.3 litre Mercedes JMO 9K at Mercedes-Benz world England. Original owner 1960/70 pop icon and influencer Donovan.

Firstly thank you for purchasing this guide. It is an accumulation of sixteen years dealing with different suppliers. I bought the classic Mercedes JMO 9K, a 1971 300 SEL 6.3 in October 2003. I then launched Barratts Classic Car Hire in 2005 after extensive work on the Mercedes was completed. I had worked on classic cars before but the Mercedes turned out to be a learning curve, mainly due to the complexity, hard to locate spares, and in general often awkward to work on design.

Over the years, I have bought and sold spares from around the world and likewise have had some parts rebuilt abroad. Restoring the car and hiring it out has given me a passport into meeting some interesting people over the years from the television, film, and music video businesses.

I quickly found out that a lot of so-called rebuild services or engine reconditioning services were just agents who would take your parts in, deliver to a reconditioning service, collect the parts or have them delivered back. Although some businesses advertise as reconditioning they are in fact just acting as a go-between.

I then spent what turned out to be many hours of telephone calls and face-to-face meetings over the years to find a reliable person or company to carry out the various different works. This was not just to save monies but to ensure that in case of problems I did not have to go through an agent. You can sometimes experience a delay going through an agent, as it depends on how helpful or efficient they are at getting your parts delivered and collected swiftly.

Over the years, people asked if I knew of where to get a car part reconditioned, or specialist service. I later decided to make all my contact information available in this guide.

I have also importantly included an established courier service that I have used extensively and have recommended. The courier service offers a vastly discounted service on major household courier names and operates worldwide door-to-door. This courier service is obviously very important, as many people reading this will not live near the companies listed or may live abroad. The courier company also operates a pallet collection and delivery service.

I have not listed bodywork or spray shops in this guide as most people can find out through clubs, etc. of a reliable bodywork company. This guide focuses on more specialist services, which are often required when carrying out maintenance or restoration work.

Classic and Vintage Car & Motorcycle Insurance in the UK

Heritage Classic Car Insurance insures tens of thousands of classic cars and specialise in both classic and vintage vehicles, cars and motorcycles as well as classic and modified 4x4s and ex-military vehicles. Established in 1965 as Norton Insurance they have built the family business and proved to be market leaders in classic car insurance. They offer free agreed value on classics, as well as discounts for car club members and a flexible multi car policy.

Personally speaking I have now used Heritage for some years as they provide the best customer service. Perhaps more importantly they have remained independent and can therefore offer very good value cover as they are not tied to one insurance company. They have in-house underwriting which means cover decisions can be made quickly and simply.

Heritage Classic Car Insurance
4 Vicarage Road
Birmingham
West Midlands
B15 3ES
England
https://bit.ly/38FqILg
Tel: + 44(0)121 248 9229

Courier Service

Those who do not live in England can also use the Company below. The courier uses some of the main worldwide courier names, which most people have heard of. The enormous difference is that they offer the same service but at a vastly discounted amount. There is nothing to pay when opening an account and the service is door-to-door.

The other good service they offer is that if you were to telephone them you do not need the internet to use their couriers. They can print off all the paperwork you need and post it to you. This printed and posted service is only available in England. For the rest of the world, you will need to have access to the internet to print off your paperwork.

The following information assumes you would like to use the internet to gain access to the paperwork. You will need an email address. If you do not have a computer and or printer this is no problem as you can go to your local library and use their public computers and printer.

You will need to measure your package as in width, height, length and, then weigh your package. You will also need the full address including any area codes of your collection address and likewise delivery address. You can book your collection and delivery online or by telephone. If you telephone there is a small charge. Once you book, the courier will email you relevant paperwork. The address document with the bar code needs to be printed, placed in a clear plastic wallet to protect it, and then firmly taped onto your package.

When the company you have used to deal with has finished your work then you will need to repeat the above procedure. This means that you will have to contact the courier and either email or post the relevant paperwork to the company.

Some companies use their own couriers. If the cost is about the same that you paid to get the package to them, you may well just agree to use their courier and save you time for the return. The company will normally add it to the monies you already owe them for the work.

You can track your package as to where it is online or by telephoning Transglobal Express.

Transglobal Express Couriers
Unit 5
The Gateway
Wirral International Business Park
Bromborough
CH62 3NX
England
www.transglobalexpress.co.uk
Tel: + 44(0)345 145 1212

Always check that what you are sending with the courier has enough insurance. Transglobal Express insure up to £2500.00 as standard. If you need to add extra insurance then Transglobal can add extra cover for a premium to save you going elsewhere. However, you may find the extra insurance at a lower cost if you were to contact this company.

The Insurance Broker
31 Chapel Hill
Longridge
Preston
Lancashire
PR3 3JY
England
www.the-insurance-broker.com
Tel: + 44(0)1772 780380

Acid Cleaning of Engine Block/Body Shell or Other Items

This Company can also acid dip a car body shell for a complete rust removal.

Surface Processing Ltd
Unit 20
Sovereign Works
Deepdale Lane
Lower Gornal
Dudley
West Midlands
DY3 2AF
England
www.surfaceprocessing.co.uk
Tel: + 44(0)1384 242010

Auto Locksmith

To have keys cut for locks where the original key has been lost, tumblers changed and keyed alike.

Auto Locksmith
Westgate
Bradford
West Yorkshire
BD1 2QL
England
Tel: + 44(0)1274 305621

Axle and Differential Rebuilding

These companies can rebuild most axles and differentials.

UK Axles
2 Fulton Close
High Wycombe
Buckinghamshire
HP13 5SP
England
www.ukaxles.co.uk
Tel: + 44(0)7738 196 468
+ 44(0)7734 169 758

Hardy Engineering Transmissions Ltd
268 Kingston Road
Leatherhead
Surrey
KT22 7QA
England
www.hardyengineering.co.uk
Tel: + 44(0)1372 378927

Battery Specialist

An excellent company who can look up the correct size that your original battery was if you have had the wrong size battery fitted. They can also supply period looking type batteries. For example, with screw-on tops whereby you used to top the battery up with distilled water.

Battery Specialist
South East Ltd
35 Dewar Road
Rainham
Kent
ME8 8DN
England
www.batteryspecialistssoutheast.co.uk
Tel: + 44(0)1634 262343

Brake Caliper Rebuilding

Although this guide does not use agents when it comes to brake caliper reconditioning most brake companies will not deal directly with the public. Brake engineering below who is one of the biggest companies in England is an example. This means that you will have to take or send your calipers to your nearest motor factors that operate the exchange or recondition service. It is very easy to find out where your nearest motor factors are by telephoning Brake Engineering below. Alternatively, you can telephone your nearest Euro Car Parts (England).

www.eurocarparts.com/store-locator
Tel: + 44(0)203 788 7842

*I used Mill Autoquip which is part of the Alliance Automotive Group. They are in Newton Abbot, Devon, England. I used them as they were very friendly and helpful. They also contact three brake exchange and reconditioning companies. This means that if one company cannot recondition your calipers then they can try two others. The other advantage is that by trying three companies they can get the best price if more than one company can help.

For people outside of England then it would be best to telephone Brake Engineering or *Mill Autoquip, Newton Abbot Devon, and ask if your calipers can be exchanged or reconditioned. If they can, then you would obviously use the courier to send your calipers to Mill Autoquip and likewise, arrange a collection by the courier.

Brake Engineering
Redwither Road
Wrexham Industrial Estate
Wrexham
LL13 9RD
England
www.brake-eng.com/en
Tel: + 44(0)1978 667810

***Mill Autoquip**
3 International House
Heathfield Industrial Estate
Battle Road
Newton Abbot
Devon
TQ12 6RY
England
www.allianceautomotive.co.uk/member/24828/mill-autoquip-newton-abbot
Tel: + 44(0)1626 333200

You can also contact the head office and ask where the nearest English Alliance Automotive dealer is to you.
www.allianceautomotive.co.uk/our-network/motor-factor-locations
Tel: + 44(0)1908 921550 head office

Carburettor Repairs and Rebuilding

Coln Engineering
Unit 3
Alma Terrace
Bristol Road
Gloucester
England
GL1 5PY
www.colnblastcleaning.co.uk
Tel: + 44(0)7791 778328

TSR Vapour Blasting
12 The Moor Road
Sevenoaks
Kent
TN14 5EB
England
www.tsrvapourblasting.co.uk
Tel: + 44(0)1732 462883

Cast Iron and Aluminium Welding, Pressure Testing & Machining

To repair cracked manifolds, engine blocks, casings, etc. Sometimes missing areas on engine blocks can be replaced with cold stitching. This involves making a mould of the missing area, casting this moulded section, and then stitching it into the main body of the surrounding metal. Once the cold stitching has been carried out the repair is hardly visible once the engine block has been painted.

It is also possible to weld in missing sections for parts such as exhaust manifolds and engine blocks, where cold stitching is not possible around broken areas, which have oil or water galleries in them.

Slinden Services Ltd
L3 Olympic House
Westminster Industrial Estate
Measham
Derbyshire
DE12 7DS
England
www.castironweldingrepairs.co.uk
Tel: + 44(0)1530 274646

Chemical Brightening

Many companies offering chemical brightening often over anodise the finished brightened trim resulting in a milky finish, which is not as bright as the factory original. The company listed in the guide anodises correctly to keep the bright finish. Mr D Roberts is the person to contact.

Colour Anodising Ltd
Holland Street
Radcliffe
Greater Manchester
M26 2RH
England
www.anodising.com
Tel: + 44 (0)161 723263

Important Information for Chemical Brightening and Polishing of Trim Sections

To explain to those who are not aware...chemical brightening is the process of brightening the trims, which are often around the front windscreen and back screen. Likewise, these trim sections are also around the doors near to the door glass or on interior door panels, etc. Many people commonly mistake these trims as being chrome plated as they look like the bright chrome finish often found on bumpers and door handles. Chemical brightening is where the trim item is dipped into a bath of hot acid which brightens the item, hence the name chemical brightening. The trim item is then anodised to protect the surface and keep it bright.

There are people or companies that sell different types of polish to bring the shine back to worn dull trims. In some cases, these cutting type polishes will work but...you will have to constantly keep polishing the trim as the cutting type polish will obviously remove the anodising, which protects the surface. These types of polish are not a permanent finish.

One important point to remember when you go to get your trim sections chemically brightened is that the trim sections need to have the anodising removed before you take or send them to be polished. Removing the anodising can easily be carried out by an anodising service such as Star Anodising or A1 anodising listed under **Zinc Plating**, on page 72.

Any anodising service would be fine for removal. The reason for removing the anodising is that it removes the hard anodised finish so that the sections can easily be polished. This is very important especially on thin delicate trim sections, as these sections need to have the least pressure put on them when polishing to avoid distortion. I have listed Dartford & Ball under **Metal Polishing**, on page 51 for polishing these delicate items. Once you have the anodising removed and trim sections polished you can then send to Colour Anodising listed under **Chemical Brightening** on page 12.

Colour Anodising can also carry out the complete service as in removing the anodising and polishing. This would save you time, but they have a minimum fee for polishing which would work out quite high if just sending a small trim section in. They send the trims to a polishing company that have aluminium fee. It depends if you would like to save time or money. I have explained both options so that readers are aware of them.

If your trim has dents in then you can of course take these to a body shop or panel beating service and enquire if they can beat the dents out. If you cannot get this done then you can use the King of Trim service listed under **Chemical Brightening and Trim Dent Removal**, on page 15. Before you send them any trims, I would strongly advise you send an image of the trim and dent. This way they can give you an indication of how much the work will cost. Trim dent removal can be expensive.

In some rare cases, the metal in the trim can alter over the years and it may be impossible to obtain a bright finish. In this case, you would have to use Ashford Chroming listed under **Chrome Plating onto Aluminium and other Metals** on page 16.

Chemical Brightening and Trim Dent Removal

This Company will carry out the complete service, anodising removal, polishing and dent removal.

King of Trim
9901 San Fernando Road
Unit 27
Pacoima
California
91331
USA
www.kingoftrim.com
Tel: (001from UK) 818 471 0279

Chrome Plating onto Aluminium and other Metals

Sometimes you may need to have aluminium parts chrome plated. A lot of chrome plating companies will not undertake aluminium to chrome plate. This company can also chrome plate many large and small automotive parts onto different metals.

Ashford Chroming
Pevington Farm
Egerton Road
Pluckley
Kent
TN27 0PF
England
www.ashfordchroming.com
Tel: + 44(0)1233 660879

Chrome Restoration for Interior and Exterior Parts

To repair dents and re-chrome on radio surrounds, trims, handles, and many automotive parts.

Mellows Eaton Ltd
Unit 5
Priestley Way
Crawley
West Sussex
RH10 9NT
England
www.mellowseatonltd.com
Tel: + 44(0)1293 532843

Clutch Plate Recorking

If you have an early cork clutch plate Vintage Supplies Ltd can re-cork it.

Vintage Supplies Ltd
Unit 7 Merebrook Business Park
Hanley Road
Malvern
Worcestershire
WR13 6NP
England
www.vintagecarparts.co.uk/products/re-cork-clutch-re-cork
Tel: + 44(0)1684 212882

Cooling Fluid

Evans lifetime cooling fluid is great for older cars as well as high-performance cars and motorcycles where overheating can be a problem, especially in the summer months when idling in traffic. Evans Coolants produce different coolants for different age vehicles so it's always best to telephone to ensure you purchase the correct cooling fluid.

This fluid is also anti-corrosion/anti-freeze and, unlike water your cooling system will not be under pressure with this fluid. This in itself is excellent as your hoses, gaskets etc are not under pressure from the coolant. In other words, you could drive around without turning down the radiator cap.

Evans has over three hundred stockists in the UK including all Euro Car Parts stores. They cover over thirty European countries, and throughout the rest of the world. They have supplied Jay Leno, the late John Surtees, and The Historic Porsche Collection.

Evans Coolants UK
Europa Way
Swansea West Business Park
Swansea
SA5 4AJ
England
www.evanscoolants.co.uk
Tel: + 44(0)1792 572299
For customers outside of the UK: ***www.evansglobal.net***

Coloured Anodising

For various different coloured anodising and other specialist finishes.

A1 Anodising Ltd
11&12 Priestley Way
Crawley
West Sussex
RH10 9NT
England
www.a1-anodising.co.uk
Tel: + 44(0)1293 539555

Star Anodising Ltd
Unit 7
Powerworks
Slade Green Road
Erith
Kent
DA8 2HY
England
www.staranodising.com
Tel: + 44(0)1322 335857

Crankshaft Straightening, Journal Repair and *Hardening

A note on crankshaft repairs

If you have a damaged crankshaft where some, or all of the journals are scored beyond grinding, and it is impossible to locate a replacement one second-hand, then the journals can be built back up with either metal spraying or submerged arc welding.

Metal spraying is a process where hot metal is sprayed onto a journal after it has been prepared. Submerged arc welding is when metal is welded onto a journal. In both cases, the repaired journals are ground back down to the correct tolerance for the bearings. Metal spraying can be carried out by T&L Engineering listed under **Engine Reconditioning Specialist, Engineering, Machining, *Welding, *Metal Spraying**, on page 32.

Metal spraying puts far less stress on a crankshaft compared to submerged arc welding. However, some views are that submerged arc welded journals are a superior job as the new metal is actually fused onto a journal by welding. Strictly speaking, a repaired crankshaft should be hardened to the same original factory original hardness.

Using hard chrome plating is often not successful for crankshaft journal repair. It is for this reason that I have not listed it.

The company below can often repair your crankshaft by submerged arc welding.

*Important

After repair work, the company below can send the crankshaft away to a specialist hardening company. When a crankshaft is re-hardened, the service is at your own risk.

The risk is that sometimes the hardening process on a repaired crankshaft can distort the crankshaft and render it useless, more so after submerged arc-welded repairs. It is for this reason that many people do not take the risk, and fit the crankshaft without surface hardening.

Coventry Boring & Metalling Co Ltd
Unit C
Hunter Terrace
Fletchworth Gate
Burnsall Road
Coventry
CV5 6SP
England
www.coventryboring.co.uk
Tel: + 44(0)2476 672372

Cylinder Head Repair

For either cast iron or aluminium cylinder heads.

Coventry Boring & Metalling Co Ltd
Unit C
Hunter Terrace
Fletchworth Gate
Burnsall Road
Coventry
CV5 6SP
England
www.coventryboring.co.uk
Tel: + 44(0)2476 672372

Electrical Ancillary Rebuild Specialist

I was impressed with this very knowledgeable company as they even had the tool to un crimp the back of the starter motor solenoid, and then re crimp back after servicing the solenoid.

Everywhere else I called upon just said "The original solenoid is not available any longer so you can only get a pattern part solenoid" this was a cheap pattern part solenoid!

Deeprose Electrical Engineers
70 Hollington Old Lane
ST Leonards on Sea
East Sussex
TN38 9DP
England
Tel: + 44(0)1424 428428

Electrical Cooling Fans

Please note

Kenlowe used to provide good quality cooling fans direct to the public. They now only supply replacements if you have already purchased one of their fans.

Please be aware that Kenlowe now supplies only the fan. There is no longer a temperature sensor or fuse carrier. Having said this it is often best to wire the fan direct via a fuse, without a temperature sensor, and just turn the fan on when needed with a switch mounted on a bracket under the dashboard out of sight. This basic set up is very reliable as obviously there is no temperature sensor to go wrong. If you still have the older style, copper capillary temperature sensor, which was in general reliable, it is good too still use it. Unfortunately, these capillary style sensors went out of production many years ago on Kenlowe fans. You could have a bracket for the switch made by T&L Engineering listed under **Engine Reconditioning Specialist, Engineering, Machining, *Welding, *Metal Spraying,** on page 32.

Due to the often-high ampere draw on the fan, you will need a fuse carrier switch and wiring sufficient to safely cope with the ampere. Often the best fuses carriers to use are the large blade type ones with bolt connections for the wires. The large blade fuse provides a good surface area for the ampere draw.

There are companies that offer low ampere cooling fans. This sounds attractive, as there is less drain on the battery and wiring. However, the trouble with these is that on many older cars, the radiators are quite thick and a low ampere fan is often not powerful enough to pass enough air through the radiator in hot weather or idling in traffic. In other words, cooling is often not sufficient.

Kenlowe Ltd
Burchetts Green Road
Burchetts Green
Maidenhead
SL6 6QU
England
www.kenlowe.com
Tel: + 44(0)1628 823303

Electronic Ignition Specialist

The American company PerTronix offer brilliant electronic ignition systems for cars, boats and agricultural machinery. They are a leading aftermarket ignition manufacturer with arguably the widest range of products and applications offering a huge selection.

I have listed their English and American dealers below. The beauty of their systems is that you do not have to drill or adapt the distributor. This is obviously very useful as if you were to sell your car and the new owner wanted to fit the original ignition system back, then this would be easy. A very friendly English service to answer any questions, with an easy to fit set up.

Although fitting the PerTronix into the distributor is easy enough, you can if you wish send your distributor to the English PerTronix listed below and ask them to fit the unit. They offer an excellent helpful service.

I have been very pleased with this excellent ignition system, as I no longer have points that can wear out and let you down, without warning. Likewise, as there are no points, there is no gap, and dwell angle to adjust. There are also no condensers to burn out and it is also possible to remove the ballast resistor when fitting PerTronix. This system delivers excellent reliability. Mr M Hannaford is the person to contact.

PerTronix Europe
1 Compton Place
Surrey Avenue
Camberley
Surrey
GU15 3DX
England
www.pertronixeurope.com/contact.php
Tel: + 44(0)1276 65554
USA Contact: ***www.pertronixbrands.com***

Engine Bearing Manufacture and Metalling

These companies manufacture engine bearings or metal your old bearings. No more worries if the bearings you require are not available through your main dealer or elsewhere.

Coventry Boring & Metalling Co Ltd
Unit C
Hunter Terrace
Fletchworth Gate
Burnsall Road
Coventry
CV5 6SP
England
www.coventryboring.co.uk
Tel: + 44(0)2476 672372

Case Engines Ltd
Stonewall Place
Silverdale
Newcastle Under Lyme
ST5 6NR
England
www.chaseengines.co.uk
Tel: + 44(0)1782 948183

Engine Bearing Suppliers

FW Thornton supply both engine and cam bearings for many engines.

FW Thornton
Orleton Lane
Wellington
Telford
Shropshire
TF1 2BG
England
www.fwthornton.co.uk
Tel: + 44(0)1952 252892

Engine Boring, Lining and Honing

Coventry Boring & Metalling Co Ltd
Unit C
Hunter Terrace
Fletchworth Gate
Burnsall Road
Coventry
CV5 6SP
England
www.coventryboring.co.uk
Tel: + 44(0)2476 672372

T+L Engineering Ltd
Unit 1
Pear Tree Farm
Wilstead Road
Elstow
Bedfordshire
MK42 9YG
England
www.vintage-engine.net
Tel: + 44(0)1234 352418

Engine Reconditioning Specialist, Engineering, Machining, *Welding and *Metal Spraying

T&L offer an excellent selection of standard and more specialist services. South Cerney is also a very established company.

They work on both car and motorcycle engines, including veteran, vintage and classic. They also work high performance engines, including dragster engines. T&L also offer a very extensive range of engineering, machining, and welding services. T&L company can sometimes also supply engine parts, which are not available elsewhere. For example, piston rings, valves, bearings, gaskets, etc.

Metal spraying is a very useful service to build up worn journals, where the part is no longer available. Sometimes damaged crankshaft journals can be metal sprayed instead of being submerged arc welded. This has the advantage of not putting the crankshaft under the same stresses of submerged arc welding.

***T+L Engineering Ltd**
Unit 1
Pear Tree Farm
Wilstead Road
Elstow
Bedfordshire
MK42 9YG
England
www.vintage-engine.net
Tel: + 44(0)1234 352418

South Cerney Engineering Ltd
Ashton Keynes
Swindon
Wiltshire
SN6 6QR
England
www.southcerneyengineering.com
Tel: + 44(0)1285 860925

Exhaust Systems

Longlife Exhaust systems are guaranteed for life (same owner, same vehicle).

Longlife Exhausts, Topgear (Bridport) Ltd.
Unit 1
Gore Business Park
Corbin Way
Bridport
Dorset
DT6 3UX
England
www.longlife.co.uk/classic-vintage-vehicles
Tel: + 44(0)1308 422282

Hayward & Scott also manufacture exhausts for boats.

Hayward & Scott
11 Nobel Square
Burnt Mills Industrial Estate
Basildon
Essex
SS13 1LS
England
www.haywardandscott.com
Tel: + 44(0)1268 727256

Fuel Tank Manufacture

Hayward & Scott manufacture aluminium and stainless steel fuel tanks.

Hayward & Scott
11 Nobel Square
Burnt Mills Industrial Estate
Basildon
Essex
SS13 1LS
England
www.haywardandscott.com
Tel: + 44(0)1268 727256

Gaskets

E Dobson gaskets are an established manufacturer of gaskets from many different types of material. M Barnwell supply many types of gasket.

E Dobson and Co [Gaskets] Ltd
Unit 1
Holme Mill Industrial Estate
Fell Lane Keighley
West Yorkshire
BD22 6BN
England
www.dobsongasket.com
Tel: +44(0)1535 607257

M Barnwell
Reginald Road
Smethwick
Birmingham
West Midlands
B67 5AS
England
www.barnwell.co.uk
Tel: +44(0)121 429 8011

Gearbox Repairs and Rebuilding

The two companies listed below specialise in transmission repair and rebuilding.

P Cheshire
Unit 8J
UBF Industrial
Westcott
Aylesbury
Buckinghamshire
HP18 0JX
England
www.pcheshire.com
Tel: +44(0)7957 974110

Automatic Gearbox Centre
Unit 3&4
Manor Industrial Estate
Newtown Road
Hove
East Sussex
BN3 7BA
England
www.automaticgearboxcentre.co.uk
Tel: +44(0)1273 722155

Gold and Silver Plating

Sometimes you may need an electrical connection gold plated.

YB Plating Ltd
Unit 6
Priestley Way
Crawley
West Sussex
RH10 9NT
England
www.ybplatingltd.co.uk
Tel: + 44(0)1293 528974

Grit Blast Cleaning, Hot Zinc Spraying and Powder Coating

A specialist blast cleaning company using different blasting grits for different services. They also offer hot zinc spray prior to powder coating or spray paint finish. They have and can blast clean from a Lighthouse to a tiny clip.

Sussex Blast Cleaning
Unit 35
Station Road Industrial Estate
Hailsham
East Sussex
BN27 2ER
England
www.sussexblastcleaning.co.uk
Tel: + 44(0)1323 849229

Hard Chroming /*Nikasil Plating & *Superfinishing

Hard chroming is a very useful service when shafts or some low stressed journals are worn and need to be built back before machining back down to an exact finish to fit in a bearing. An example of this would be a steering column.

Nikasil is short for Nickel Silicon Carbide. It is a nickel and silicon (ceramic) plating which is very hard. This is used mainly for providing a very hard wearing surface on the inside of aluminium cylinder bores. In some cases over the years it has replaced hard chroming.

TSR undertake Nikasil plating as well as Superfinishing which involves a superior surface finish which can extend the life of parts, especially gears.

Yorkshire Plating Services
Unit 16/17
Alma Works
Bradford
BD4 8QE
England
www.yorkshireplating.co.uk
Tel: + 44(0)1274 651148

***TSR Vapour Blasting**
12 The Moor Road
Sevenoaks
Kent
TN14 5EB
England
www.tsrvapourblasting.co.uk
Tel: + 44(0)1732 462883

Hydraulic Hose Manufacture

Many car or motorcycle dealers no longer supply hydraulic hoses with the correct angled union tales for older models. This means that you will have to have the union tales cut off your old hose and brazed into new hose connections. The hose company below will do all of this. If the original hose connections were yellow or silver zinc plated then you can purchase the hose connections with newly brazed in sections and send them away to be zinc plated. Once zinc plated you can then get the complete hose made.

Phoenix Contracts Ltd
Unit 1
Trinity Trading Estate
Tribune Drive
Sittingbourne
ME10 2PG
England
Tel: + 44(0)1795 420594

Instrument Cluster Repairs

Clocks, Speedometer, Tachometer, Gauges, etc.

Please note

If you have the old style of time clock which was fitted before the quartz movement was introduced then it is often a waste of time sending these clocks off to have the time set accurately. It is common for these old-style mechanisms for not keeping an accurate time after a few years from new as the parts wear. It is therefore often impossible to have these clocks set to keep accurate time for any long period.

Unfortunately, most of these clocks parts are no longer available to repair them. It is also often a waste of time buying another second-hand clock thinking that you can use the parts to try and make one good clock.....Do not forget that the clock you will be buying will more than likely suffer from the same worn parts!

It is sometimes possible to get a clock converted to a quartz movement all inside the original case.

JDO Instruments
34 Spring Avenue
Keighley
West Yorkshire
BD21 4UG
England
www.jdo1.com
Tel: + 44(0)1535 672125
+ 44(0)7831 886545

Instrument Cluster Repairs and Cable Building

For nearly all gauge repairs and cable building.

Speedometer Service Company
5801 W Villard Avenue
Milwaukee
WI 53218
USA
www.speedometersolutions.com
Tel: (001from UK) 414 463 6660

Laser Welding

This specialist welding service can really get you out of a problem when it comes to repairing casings or heaver items. The laser is such an intense focused heat that there is often no distortion.

I have used this service to repair small dents on the tops of pistons, and repair a delicate aluminium speedometer cable housing.

Carrs Laser Technologies Ltd
Unit 2
Henson Park
Telford Way Industrial Estate
Kettering
NN16 8PX
England
www.carrswelding.co.uk
Tel: + 44(0)1536 412828

Leather

This is an established well-known and respected English firm of many years supplying hides for many high-end applications, including the aviation industry.

Many people have heard of Connolly leather. When it comes to leather, other companies may say that they can save you money and supply a period leather to match for less than Connolly's charge. What they do not tell you is that they are agents who often purchase cheap leather and try to pass it off as being virtually the same as Connolly hide. Most of this cheap leather is generally thin poor quality.

If you have a question and would like proper advice, contact Connolly Brothers. They can supply the older style of vegetable-dyed leather. You can send them a sample of your leather to match up. They offer an excellent friendly advice service for whatever application you require the leather. You can purchase from Connolly Brothers or from one of their agents if nearer to you. For customers outside of England, before you look elsewhere you would be best advised to contact Connolly Brothers first and send them a sample as they can often supply the correct leather you require at a lower cost than other suppliers/agents.

Mr Ben Connolly
Connolly Brothers
Unit 1
Spelmonden Estate
Spelmonden
Kent
TN17 1HE
England
www.connollybros.co.uk
Tel: + 44(0)1580 213622

Aeristo leather
2550 N
Great Southwest Parkway
Grand Prairie
Texas 75050
USA
www.aeristo.com
Tel: (001 from UK) 817 624 8400
USA Toll Free – 1 800 736 6201

Leather, Cloth and Vinyl

GAHH can also make seat covers from patterns they hold.

GAHH Automotive
11128 Gault Street
North Hollywood
CA 91605
USA
www.gahh.com
Tel: (001 from UK) 818 767 6242
818 432 3757

Magneto Repairs and Rebuilding

The Magneto Guys are specialists and also rebuild aircraft and boat magnetos which a lot of other magneto companies will not repair or rebuild.

The Magneto Guys
Hailsham
East Sussex
England
www.themagnetoguys.co.uk
Tel: + 44(0)1323 840203

Armoto Ltd
Unit 26
M1 Commerce Park
Markham Lane
Duckmanton
Chesterfield
S44 5HS
England
www.vehicle-electrical-rewinds.co.uk
Tel: + 44(0)1246 826667

Dave Lindsley Magnetos - FOR MOTORCYCLE MAGNETOS ONLY
(Unfortunately this company does not trade with USA and Canada)
Unit 22
Evans Business Centre (now FLEXSPACE)
Enterprise Park
Brunel Road
Leominster
Herefordshire
HR6 OLX
England
www.davelindsley.co.uk
Tel: + 44(0)1568 617750

Mechanical Fuel Injection Pump Repair, Spares and *Ultra Sonic Cleaning

Tower Bridge Diesels
The Crossways
East Ravendale
Grimsby
DN37 0RX
England
www.towerbridgediesels.co.uk
Tel: + 44(0)1472 827632
Mob: + 44(0)7944 977711

***TSR Vapour Blasting**
12 The Moor Road
Sevenoaks
Kent
TN14 5EB
England
www.tsrvapourblasting.co.uk
Tel: + 44(0)1732 462883

Mercedes-Benz Classic Parts

There are companies in Germany, which will also recondition the same parts as Star Motors...but I have always found Star Motors to be a quicker service with obviously no language barrier, and likewise fairer with what they charge.

Examples, air suspension valves, air suspension compressor, front subframe with air chambers etc.

Star Motors
1694 Union Center Highway
Endicott
New York
1370- 1341
USA
www.300sel.com
Tel: (001 from UK) 607 786 3918

Metal Hardening Services

These specialist companies use different hardening methods. They can harden crankshafts etc. Please see their advice and *Important under **Crankshaft Straightening, Journal Repair and *Hardening** on page 21 with reference to hardening on repaired crankshafts.

Summitglow Ltd
45 Harleston Street
Sheffield
S4 7QB
England
www.summitglow.co.uk
Tel: + 44(0)114 270 186

CBS Engineering & Heat Treatment Ltd
Acton Grove
Long Eaton
Nottingham
NG10 1FY
England
www.cbsengineeringuk.co.uk/heat-treatment
Tel: + 44(0)115 946 0011

Metal Polishing

There are many very good polishing companies around. However, finding a company that can polish thin delicate trims that can bend easily is often difficult. The company below can polish from thick large areas down to very small thin fragile soft aluminium sections that many polishing companies would not work on. This is a vital service prior to having sections chemically brightened. If the trim section is not polished, then you will not be able to achieve a bright finish. Sometimes delicate trims can be taped onto a board for polishing to avoid distortion.

Whenever I have sent these delicate sections of trim through a courier, I have made a strong wooden crate from plywood. The crate is then screwed back down and couriered back to you with your polished trims. If the trims are straight, you could use plastic plumbing waste pipe to transport them in.

Dartford and Ball Polishers Ltd
Unit 7
Kennet Road
Dartford
Kent
DA1 4QN
England
Tel: + 44(0)1322 554338

Number Plate Manufacture

Established in 1932 Tippers manufacturer number plates for all types of vehicle.

Tippers Number Plates
Unit 2
Bucklers Lane
St Austell
PL25 3JN
England
www.tippersvintageplates.co.uk
Tel: +44(0)1726 879799

Piston and Piston Ring Suppliers

The first two companies listed below supply both pistons and piston rings.

The last company M Barnwell supply piston rings.

FW Thornton
Orleton Lane
Wellington
Telford
Shropshire
TF1 2BG
England
www.fwthornton.co.uk
Tel: + 44(0)1952 252892

Cox & Turner Engineering
Huish Farm
Yeovil Road
Tintinhull
Yeovil
Somerset
BA22 8QL
England
www.coxandturner.co.uk
Tel: +44(0)7377 366214

M Barnwell
Reginald Road
Smethwick
Birmingham
West Midlands
B67 5AS
England
www.barnwell.co.uk
Tel: +44(0)121 429 8011

Power and Manual Steering Rack Reconditioning & Repair

Power Steering Box and Pump Reconditioning & Repair

If your power steering box, pump, or rack is leaking and or defective then this company can rebuild. Manual steering racks can also be rebuilt.

Kelly Bray Steering
Florence Road
Kelly Bray
Callington
Cornwall
PL17 8EF
England
www.kellybraysteering.co.uk
Tel: + 44(0)1579 382766

Radiator Repairs and Re-core

In most cases, you do not need to discard the whole radiator but instead have, the main core replaced and any dents knocked out of the brass cases surrounding the core.

Vintage Car Radiator Company
Building 99 B+C
Buckingham Road
Bicester
Oxfordshire
OX26 5HA
England
www.vintagecarradiatorcompany.co.uk
Tel: + 44(0)1869 240001

Radio Spares and Repairs

A very useful service for classic Blaupunkt and Becker radios.

Classic Blaupunkt and Becker
New York
USA
www.vintageblau.com
Tel: (001 from UK) 631 697 1611

Seal Manufacture and PTFE Packing

Sealmasters are an established seal specialist who arrange seal manufacture from different types of material. Viton is considered the strongest for many oil and hydraulic seals.

Sealmasters Ltd
Unit 4
Metalcraft Court
Seawalls Road Cardiff
CF24 5TH
England
www.sealmasters.co.uk
Tel: + 44(0)2920 490711

Spark Plug Caps, Spark Plugs, HT lead, Coils

This company stocks Beru, Bosch, Champion products.

Sparkplugs.co.uk
Unit 4H
Chester
Cheshire
CH4 8RQ
England
www.sparkplugs.co.uk
Tel: + 44(0)1244 679903

For specialist spark plugs and many accessories including dynamos and starter motors.

The Green Spark Plug Company
Unit 2
King Street Trading Estate
Middlewich
Cheshire
CW10 9LF
England
https://tidd.ly/3z5Nw4s
Tel: + 44(0)1477 532317

Trim Repairs

This excellent company below can repair many types of trim to a virtually invisible finish. From damage caused by wear and tear, screw holes, splits, cigarette burns, and stone chips nearly all interior and exterior trim can be repaired. For example dashboards, carpet repairs, door trim repairs, exterior trim and bumpers, interior trim.

They also repair chips in windscreens and generally operate around the Northampton area in England, whereby they come out and repair. In common with most other businesses listed in the guide, you can use the courier to send trim items to them for repair.

They are planning to open up in the USA in the future, starting around the Pittsburgh area.

Trimperfect
The Old Stone House
Great Billing
Northampton
NN3 9BL
England
www.trimperfect.co.uk
Mob: + 44(0)7765 402643

Trimming Services

The two companies below carry out a wide range of trimming services for cars, motorcycles, boats, aeroplanes, etc.

AS Pickering Ltd
7 Springfield Place
Springfield Works
Bradford
BD1 3EZ
England
www.aspickering.co.uk
Tel: + 44(0)1274 724000

SM Trimming
Merlins
Clayhill
East Sussex
BN8 5RU
England
www.smtrimming.co.uk
Tel: + 44(0)1273 813444

Trimming Supplies

This trimming materials company can supply leather by the square foot on their stock leathers. Most trimmers will either normally charge you for a half or full hide. This can be useful if you do not require particular period leather.

Aldridge Trimming Ltd
Castle House
Drayton Street
Wolverhampton
West Midlands
WV2 4EF
England
www.aldridge.co.uk
Tel: + 44(0)1902 710805

Trim and Upholstery Supplies, Custom Colour Leather Dyes & Custom Colour Vinyl Paint

This very useful company supply a very comprehensive range of products for mainly English vintage and classic cars. Examples: trims, window channelling, door panel clips, carpet and trim studs, door and boot seals, hood materials, headlining, foil-backed heat insulation, sound-insulating felt, millboard, foam sheeting, hessian, piping's, calico, rubber sheeting, woven bonnet tape, many black rubber extrusions, screws, bonnet catches, grab handles, door locks, window handles, clevis pins, emblems, carpets, gasket materials, windscreen universal fitting tool, brass taps, and fittings. Even an Aeroscreen suitable for RAC competition. They also mix custom colour leather dye and vinyl paint.

Woollies Ltd
Whitley Way
Northfields Industrial Estate
Market Deeping
Peterborough
PE6 8AR
England
www.woolies-trim.co.uk
Tel: + 44(0)1778 341847

Turbocharger Repairs and Re-building

Turboworks Ltd
Unit 1B
16A Maple Road
Eastbourne
East Sussex
BN23 6NY
England
www.turboworks.co.uk
Tel: +44(0)1323 301999

Tyres

For specialist tyres that local tyre companies cannot supply.

Vintage Tyres
The National Motor Museum
Beaulieu
Southamton
SO42 7ZN
England
www.vintagetyres.com
Tel: + 44(0)1590 612261

Valves and Valve Guide Suppliers

The two established companies supply valves, valve guides/springs for many different engines.

FW Thornton
Orleton Lane
Wellington
Telford
Shropshire
England
TF1 2BG
England
www.fwthornton.co.uk
Tel: + 44(0)1952 252892

Cox & Turner Engineering
Huish Farm
Yeovil Road
Tintinhull
Yeovil
Somerset
BA22 8QL
England
www.coxandturner.co.uk
Tel: +44(0)7377 366214

Vapour Blasting/Wet blasting

Vapour blasting has become increasingly popular over the years, as more people are using this process to keep mainly aluminium sections clean. Other non-ferrous metals such as brass, copper, and including stainless steel can also be vapour blasted.

To explain to those who are not aware...vapour blasting or wet blasting as it is sometimes referred to be is when aluminium is blasted with grit and water. This has the effect of smoothing off the aluminium and providing a shiny finish. The main advantage of this is that oil and dirt wipe off the surface unlike a normal cast finish, which traps particles of dirt and oil.

T+L Engineering Ltd
Unit 1
Pear Tree Farm
Wilstead Road
Elstow
Bedfordshire
MK42 9YG
England
www.vintage-engine.net
Tel: + 44(0)1234 352418

TSR Vapour Blasting
12 The Moor Road
Sevenoaks
Kent
TN14 5EB
England
www.tsrvapourblasting.co.uk
Tel: + 44(0)1732 462883

Water and Hydraulic Pipes Angled to Shape

If you have a water pipe that has corroded and is not available anymore, then you can take or courier your rotted pipe to the company below who can then bend the new steel or another metal pipe to the same shape.

In some cases, you will have to get a spigot or flange welded onto the new pipe by a local engineering firm or T&L Engineering listed earlier. Sometimes if corrosion-free, it is possible to cut the flange or spigot off your old pipe and have welded onto the new pipe. If the flange or spigot is corroded then the engineering works will have to make up a new flange and spigot. Once all this is finished you could then get the new pipe zinc plated. **Zinc Plating** is listed on page 72.

Tubesmiths (southern) Ltd
Sedlescombe Sawmills
Cripps Corner
Robertsbridge
East Sussex
TN32 5SA
England
Tel: + 44(0)1580 830770

Water Pump Rebuilding

An established company specialising in the remanufacture of car, truck, bus, plant, agricultural, marine and industrial water pumps. Extensive stocks of new water pumps are also carried.

SP Water Pumps Ltd
6 Tatton Court
Kingsland Grange
Woolston
Warrington
Cheshire
WA1 4RR
England
www.spwaterpumps.co.uk
Tel: + 44(0)1925 850082

Wire Wheel Repair and Restoration

For wire wheels, steel and alloy rims, hub restoration and manufacture.

Turrino Wheels Ltd
Units 8/9
Elliott's Yard
Park Street
Kings Cliffe
Peterborough
PE8 6ER
England
www.turrinowirewheels.com
Tel: + 44(0)1780 470460

Wiring Looms and Accessories Suppliers & Services

Electrical Car Services
Essex
England
www.electricalcarservices.com
Tel: + 44(0)1268 778342
Mob: + 44(0)7710 945405

Mendip Auto Electrical
Netherleigh
Ham Lane
Paulton
Bristol
Avon
BS39 7QP
England
www.mendipautoelectrical.co.uk
Mob: + 44(0)7702 133212

Autosparks Ltd
80-88 Derby Road
Sandiacre
Nottingham
NG10 5HU
England
www.autosparks.co.uk
Tel: + 44(0)115 949 7211

Wood Repair and Finishing

For the repair or restoration of wooden dashboards and other trim.

Nick Martin
Spalding
Linconshire
PE11 2LD
England
www.nicholas-martin.co.uk
Mob: + 44(0)7977 741889

Zinc Plating

I have often used both the companies below, especially YB Plating as they can often turn work around quicker than many other companies can. YB is also more used to receiving customer's items through the post.

All three companies operate other plating services apart from zinc plating.

YB Plating Ltd
Unit 6
Priestley Way
Crawley
West Sussex
RH10 9NT
England
www.ybplatingltd.co.uk
Tel: + 44(0)1293 528974

Yorkshire Plating Services
Unit 16/17
Alma Works
Bradford
BD4 8QE
England
www.yorkshireplating.co.uk
Tel: + 44(0)1274 651148

Star Anodising Ltd
Unit 7
Powerworks
Slade Green Road
Erith
Kent
DA8 2HY
England
www.staranodising.com
Tel: + 44(0)1322 335857

Farewell Points Hello PerTronix

Reliable Easy to Fit PerTronix Electronic Ignition.

For many when restoring a period car keeping things as original as possible is often important. However, I believe along with many other restorers that you should also balance originality out against function ability. This very much applies to the all-important ignition system.

As most, vintage and classic car owners are aware; points are often a weak link in the ignition system and can suddenly let you down. Veteran cars generally had magneto ignition. Around the early 1980s coil boosters were often fitted to improve the spark, but of course, you still had the points which could start to deteriorate through spark erosion, more so if the condenser had started to fail.

There are various electronic ignition systems on the market and some use light as the sensing method. These, in general, are ok, but if any dirt or grease gets on the light it can let you down.

Electronic ignition systems which work off of a magnet are often more reliable. The beauty of the PerTronix system is that it is so simple, one of those cases in life where less is more. Fitting this type of ignition is often a simple operation. Another beauty of this system is that, once it is fitted there is no longer any dwell angle to adjust. The electronic ignition uses a hall sensor which is switched by another circular magnet which fits under the rotor arm.

Lower image: Top view of PerTronix ignitor and trigger magnet, with both sets of points and intermediate base plate removed.

Another advantage of this magnet ignition system is that there are no drilling or permanent modifications to the distributor. Likewise, there are no electronic boxes to be fitted in the engine bay. In general, different ignition systems are available for most models of a distributor. In some cases where a distributor has two sets of points, you can discard both sets of points, condenser and ballast resistor. The intermediate distributor base plate can sometimes be removed as well. All these items along with their screws and clips can be stored away so that if you ever want to return the car to its original set up it can be easily be carried out. If you remove the ballast resistor then you should replace the coil with one from PerTronix, as the PerTonix coil provides resistant protection to the ignition system. Apart from fitting the new ignition system it is essential to check for wear in the distributor cap, rotor arm, HT leads and caps. It is a good idea to replace these items at the same time if they are old and worn. Spark plugs should of course also be checked.

Fitting these magnet electronic ignition systems to older cars is a very good idea as it greatly increases the reliability of the ignition system. Once fitted you will often notice the engine is slightly more responsive. You will of course no longer have to replace the sometimes costly points or condenser. Obviously, there is no risk of the points letting you down as they are no longer fitted. It is also a good idea to fit a PerTronix upgraded coil to produce a better spark. There are claims that an upgraded coil will help make the engine a little more economical due to the increased spark size and hence better combustion.

Some people reading this may well have already heard of PerTronix as they are a market leader in electronic ignition and some Members may well have fitted their systems. This article is primarily for those who have not. PerTronix also offers a fitting service if you send them your distributor.

Many years ago I spoke to a contact of mine, who said that a German contact of his had been fitting the PerTronix systems for a while with no problems. After a little research, I decided to purchase this system for my classic Mercedes. The beauty of this system is that it is so simple, one of those cases in life where less is more. It is almost comical when you open the small PerTronix ignitor box – there is hardly anything there. Fitting the ignitor is a simple operation. The instructions provided are clear and simple with easy to follow diagrams, and there is excellent, friendly service from Mark Hannaford of PerTronix should you have any queries. Another beauty of this system is that, once it is fitted, there is no longer any dwell angle to adjust. The PerTronix ignitor uses a hall sensor which is switched by another circular magnet which fits under the rotor arm. Once fitted, there are no ongoing adjustments to make inside the distributor.

A great selling point of these systems is that there is no drilling or permanent modifications to the distributor required, or electronic boxes to be fitted in the engine bay. When I fitted the PerTronx to my classic Mercedes I was able to discard both sets of points, intermediate distributor base plate and condenser. I also purchased the high-energy (*Flame-Thrower*) coil which enabled the ballast resistor to be removed, as the coil had the resistance built-in. You can put all the original items, along with their screws and clips, safely away so that if you ever want to return the car to its original set up it can be easily done.

Lower image: Side view of PerTronix ignitor and trigger magnet, with both sets of points and intermediate base plate removed.

Once I fitted the system I noticed the engine was slightly more responsive – and I will no longer have to replace the points or condenser or run the risk of them letting me down. In my opinion, if you fit the Flame-Thrower coil, the PerTronix system also makes the engine a little more economical – due to the increased spark size and hence better combustion. PerTronix also makes this point in their advertising.

If you do not have good timing light, i.e. one that gives a good white light, then you can purchase the Draper TL3 timing light. This is available from motor factors or on-line stores. I purchased it and am very pleased with it. You can easily see the bright white light on the crankshaft pulley during daylight. The quality of the light is comparable with those found in far more expensive units. You will also need a good tachometer to set the engine idle speed to make sure the timing is correct, but if you have not got these are fairly inexpensive to purchase.

You may encounter a small amount of needle bounce from the dashboard tachometer; this is a result of the extra sharp signal from the ignitor and is nothing to worry about. If you wish to remove the bounce then you can fit a 50,000-ohm resistor which should be wired into the connection on the negative side of the coil. To make this a neat quality job I soldered the 50,000-ohm resistor onto a wire each side. I then soldered the wire ends onto to *ring connectors. I lastly covered all the resistor and wiring in shrink wrap, just leaving the two ring connector ends exposed for connection. This way the section of wiring that has just been made can simply be bolted one end onto the wiring loom which was previously bolted to the coil. The other end of the wiring then of course bolts onto the negative side of the coil. This way you are not cutting into or altering the standard wiring loom connections. On some vehicles, it may be possible to adjust the tachometer internally to stop the bounce.

*Ring connectors may not be fitted. Some wiring looms use the spade connectors or other connectors.

Mr M Hannaford
PerTronix Europe
1 Compton Place
Surrey Avenue
Camberley
Surrey
GU15 3DX
England
www.pertronixeurope.com/contact.php
Tel: + 44(0)1276 65554

USA Contact: ***www.pertronixbrands.com***

www.ingramcontent.com/pod-product-compliance
Ingram Content Group UK Ltd.
Pitfield, Milton Keynes, MK11 3LW, UK
UKHW020415250726
13967UKWH00007B/2659